At the [illegible]ge

Edited by Sue Hackman

Hodder Murray

A MEMBER OF THE HODDER HEADLINE GROUP

Hodder Headline's policy is to use papers that are natural, renewable and recyclable products and made from wood grown in sustainable forests. The logging and manufacturing processes are expected to conform to the environmental regulations of the country of origin.

Orders: please contact Bookpoint Ltd, 130 Milton Park, Abingdon, Oxon OX14 4SB. Telephone: (44) 01235 827720. Fax: (44) 01235 400454. Lines are open from 9.00am to 5.00pm, Monday to Saturday, with a 24-hour message answering service.
Visit our website at www.hoddereducation.co.uk

First published in the Hodder Reading Project series in 2006 by Hodder Murray, an imprint of Hodder Education, a member of the Hodder Headline Group, 338 Euston Road, London NW1 3BH.

Impression number	10 9 8 7 6 5 4 3 2 1
Year	2011 2010 2009 2008 2007 2006

Cover photo: ImagineThat/Alamy.
Typeset in Bembo by Servis Filmsetting Limited, Manchester.
Printed in Great Britain by Cox & Wyman Ltd, Reading, Berkshire.

A catalogue record for this title is available from the British Library

ISBN-10: 0 340 91563 3
ISBN-13: 978 0340 915 639

Contents

On the Roof of the World

Mountaineering adventures

1
Sickness at 13,000 feet

Mountaineering can be a dangerous sport, and not just because of the climbing. High up, the air is thin and climbers can get altitude sickness. Jonathan Waterman describes how he climbed to the summit of Mount McKinley in Alaska in 1982, suffering from altitude sickness.

As the climbing became less difficult we grew weaker from the altitude. The thermometer read forty below. Though we wore every piece of clothing we had, the wind came right through our customized suits.

Stomach acid clung to the back of my throat. After a brief rest, panting over my ice-axe, I raced upward with a pulse drumming in my head.

Up, up we went. The tempo of the drumbeat increased in my head. My feet turned leaden. I could not find a rhythm, let alone go more than one step at a time. Mike and Roger yelled for me to hurry up but I could barely move, so after cursing they pulled gear out of my pack to lighten my load. Still, I stumbled back and forth, woozy with thin air.

Finally, after a paltry thousand feet, they stopped and chopped a platform. When I arrived, their anger hung like the calm before a great storm. They could have gone on to the top. Bivouacs* this high on the mountain were foolhardy, maybe even deadly. But short of being dragged I could not go on.

We piled into the tent. I was too weak to talk. My world spun and dipped and hovered as I held my head and tried to catch my breath. Mike plied me with tea while Roger looked out the door and analyzed the sky; they took turns looking out the tent as if something were coming to get us. I'll never forget their wide eyes, the creases on their foreheads, the tension that shook the tent like the wind. Even sick, I knew how worried and scared and tiny we were.

I had destroyed our speedy climb, so I closed my eyes and let sickness spin away from the bitter realities into unconsciousness. That night the tent became a frozen coffin. We tossed and turned and rolled onto each other throughout the long, long night.

Just before the dawn I dreamed of drowning. I came alive thrashing and lunging for my sleeping-bag zipper, desperate for air. I sat up and realized that fluid had infiltrated my lungs; I could only steal panting breaths.

While the stove roared, Mike changed socks. His two big toes were black with frostbite, but when Roger peered closer, Mike yanked the socks back on. 'Oh,' he said, 'it's nothing.'

Stuffing my sleeping bag seemed to take hours. After breakfast, they left the tent, so I zipped the door

* **Bivouac:** tent

Mount McKinley is North America's highest mountain.

shut, steepled my hands together, and begged for good weather and the strength to survive the coming ordeal.

Mike overheard me. He knew. 'You say something, Jon?'

'No,' I said, my breath bubbling. 'Nothing.'

I followed their steps, oblivious to the sea of clouds that had arrived, oblivious to the passage of time, and acutely aware of the terrible heaviness of gravity that repeatedly sent me sprawling to the snow.

After several hours, Mike and Roger dropped their packs, and walked the fifty yards to the summit. When they returned, they were not amused to see me crawling down below.

Mike jogged down and relieved me of my pack. Twenty minutes later, I finished my crawl to the summit ridge. I looked briefly upward, but on this day my success would be measured in survival, not a summit. I could manage only two steps before collapsing over my axe and fighting for the privilege of breathing. The wind was mild but the cold was vivid, and despite wearing three sets of layered mittens we couldn't touch our metal-topped axes. Somehow it registered that my toes had frozen.

I had to pace myself, breathe twice for each step, then rest for ten breaths. Again, again, and again. I forced myself into the rhythm, eyes locked on my feet. It became a game: how do you move forward when you can barely breathe?

From 'Aurora' by Jonathan Waterman

2
Accident on Annapurna

Maurice Herzog climbed Annapurna with a team of French climbers in 1950. The team included local climbing experts, the Sherpas. At the time, it was the highest mountain ever climbed. The way down proved to be harder than the way up.

Then the descent began.

It is said that mountaineers have a sixth sense that warns them of danger – suddenly I became aware of danger through every pore of my body. There was a feeling in the atmosphere that could not be ignored. Yesterday it had snowed heavily, and the heat was now working on these great masses of snow which were on the point of sliding off. Nothing in Europe can give any idea of the force of these avalanches. They roll down over a distance of miles and are preceded by a blast that destroys everything in its path.

The glare was so terrific that without glasses it would have been impossible to keep one's eyes open. By good luck we were fairly well spaced out, so that the risk was diminished. The Sherpas no longer remembered the different pitches, and often with great difficulty, I had to take the lead and be let down on the end of the rope to find the right way. I had no crampons[1] and I could not grasp an axe. We lost height far too slowly for my liking, and it worried me to see my Sherpas going so slowly and carefully and at the same time so insecurely. In actual fact they went very well, but I was so impatient I could no longer judge their performance fairly.

Lachenal was a long way behind us and every time I turned around he was sitting down in the track. He, too, was affected by snow-blindness, though not as badly as Terray and Rébuffat, and found difficulty in seeing his way. Rébuffat went ahead by guess-work, with agony in his face, but he kept on. We crossed the couloir[2] without incident, and I congratulated myself that we had passed the danger zone.

The sun was at its height, the weather brilliant, and the colours magnificent. Never had the mountains appeared to me so majestic as in this moment of extreme danger.

All at once a crack appeared in the snow under the feet of the Sherpas, and grew longer and wider. A mad

[1] **Crampon:** spike on the sole of a boot
[2] **Couloir:** steep narrow gully or crack in the mountainside

notion flashed into my head – to climb up the slope and reach solid ground. Then I was lifted up by a superhuman force, and as the Sherpas disappeared before my eyes, I went head over heels. I could not see what was happening. My head hit the ice. In spite of my efforts I could no longer breathe, and a violent blow on my left thigh caused me acute pain. I turned round and round like a puppet. In a flash I saw the blinding light of the sun through the snow which was pouring past my eyes. The rope joining me to Sarki and Aila curled round my neck – the Sherpas shooting down the slope beneath would shortly strangle me, and the pain was unbearable. Again and again I crashed into solid ice as I went hurtling from one serac* to another, and the snow crushed me down. The rope tightened around my neck and brought me to a stop. Before I had recovered my wits I began to pass water, violently and uncontrollably.

I opened my eyes, to find myself hanging head downwards, with the rope around my neck and my left leg, in a sort of hatchway of blue ice. I put out my elbows towards the walls in an attempt to stop the unbearable pendulum motion which sent me from one side to the other, and caught a glimpse of the final slopes beneath me. My breathing steadied, and I blessed the rope which had stood the strain of the shock.

I simply *had* to try to get myself out. My feet and hands were numb, but I was able to make use of some little nicks in the wall. There was room for at least the edges of my boots. By frenzied, jerky movements

* Serac: ridge of ice

I succeeded in freeing my left leg from the rope, and then managed to right myself and to climb up a yard or two. After every move I stopped, convinced that I had come to the end of my physical strength, and that in a second I should have to let go.

One more desperate effort, and I gained a few more inches – I pulled on the rope and felt something give at the other end – no doubt the bodies of the Sherpas. I called, but hardly a whisper issued from my lips. There was a death-like silence. Where was Gaston?

Conscious of a shadow, as from a passing cloud, I looked up instinctively; and lo and behold! two scared faces were framed against the circle of blue sky. Aila and Sarki! They were safe and sound, and at once set to work to rescue me. I was incapable of giving them the slightest advice. Aila disappeared, leaving Sarki alone at the edge of the hole; they began to pull on the rope, slowly, so as not to hurt me, and I was hauled up with a power and steadiness that gave me fresh courage. At last I was out. I collapsed on the snow.

The rope had caught over a ridge of ice and we had been suspended on either side; by good luck the weight of the two Sherpas and my own had balanced. If we had not been checked like this we should have hurtled down another 1,500 ft.

From 'Annapurna, Mon Amour'
by Maurice Herzog

3
Frost-bite

One of Maurice Herzog's worst memories of climbing was getting frost-bite. Frost-bite can kill. It freezes and kills off the flesh. If it is treated quickly, it can be cured by getting blood to circulate again in the frozen arm or leg, but if it is left too long the limb must be amputated.

Everyone was now off the mountain and assembled at Camp II. But in what a state! Oudot made a rapid tour of inspection.

He examined me first. My limbs were numb up to well beyond the ankles and wrists. My hands were in a frightful condition; there was practically no skin left. The little that remained was black, and long strips dangled down. My fingers were both swollen and distorted. My feet were scarcely any better: the entire soles were brown and violet, and completely without feeling. The arm which was hurting me, and which I was afraid might be broken, did not appear to be seriously injured, and my neck was all right.

I was anxious to have Oudot's first impression.

'What do you think of it all?' I asked him, ready to hear the worst.

'It's pretty serious. You'll probably lose part of your feet and hands. At present I can't say more than that.'

'Do you think you'll be able to save something?'

'Yes, I'm sure of it. I'll do all I can.'

This was not encouraging, and I was convinced that my feet and hands would have to be amputated.

Oudot took my blood pressure and seemed rather concerned. There was no pressure in the right arm, and the needle did not respond at all on my left arm. On my legs the needle oscillated slightly, indicating a restricted flow of blood. After putting a dressing over my eyes to prevent ophthalmia, he said:

'I'm going to see Lachenal. I'll come back in a moment and give you some injections. I used them during the war and it's the only treatment that's any use with frost-bite. See you presently.'

Night fell gradually. Oudot made his preparations, and Camp II was turned into a hospital. In cold and discomfort, and to the accompaniment of continual avalanches, these men fought, late into the night, to save their friends. Armed with torches, they passed from tent to tent, bending over the wounded and giving them emergency treatment, at this minute camp, perched 20,000 feet up on the flanks of one of the highest mountains in the world.

Oudot made ready to give me injections. The lamp shone feebly and in the semi-darkness Ichac sterilized the syringes as best he could with ether. Before starting, Oudot explained:

'I am going to inject novocaine into your femoral and brachial arteries.'

As I could not see a thing with the bandage over my eyes, he touched with his finger the places where he would insert the needle: both groins and in the bends of my elbows.

'It's going to hurt. Perhaps I shan't get the right place first shot. But in any case you mustn't move, particularly when I have got into the artery.'

I was not at all reassured by these preparations; I had always had a horror of injections. But it would have to be done, it was the only thing possible.

'Go ahead,' I said to Oudot, 'but warn me when you are going to stab.'

Anyhow, perhaps it would not hurt all that much in my present condition. I heard the murmur of voices – Oudot asking if something was ready, and Ichac answering: 'Here you are. Got it?'

Oudot ran his fingers over my skin. I felt an acute pain in my groin and my legs began to tremble; I tried to control myself. He had to try again, for the artery had rolled away from the needle. Another stab, and my whole body was seized with convulsions, I stiffened when I should have relaxed, and felt all my nerves in revolt.

'Gently!' I could not help myself.

Oudot began again: my blood was extremely thick and clotted in the needle.

'You're blood is black – it's like black pudding,' he said in amazement.

'That's got it!' This time he had succeeded in spite of my howls which, I knew very well, made the operation all the more difficult to perform. The needle was now in position:

'Don't move!' Oudot shouted at me. Then to Ichac: 'Hand it over!'

Ichac passed him the syringe; I felt the needle moving in my flesh and the liquid began to flow into the artery. I should never, until then, have believed so much pain to be possible. I tried to brace myself to the utmost to keep myself from trembling: it simply had to be successful! The liquid went on flowing in.

'Can you feel any warmth?' asked Oudot, brusquely, while he was changing the syringe. Again the liquid went in; I gritted my teeth.

'Does it feel warm?'

Oudot was insistent – the point was evidently crucial; yet still I felt nothing. Several times the syringe was emptied, filled up, and emptied again:

'Now, do you feel anything?'

'I seem to feel a little warmth, but it's not very definite.'

Was it auto-suggestion? The needle was withdrawn abruptly, and while Ichac sterilized the instruments, I had a few moments' respite.

'It's excruciating, the way it hurts,' I said, just as if Oudot needed telling!

'Yes, I know, but we must go on.'

The performance was repeated on the other leg. My nerves were all to pieces, and to brace myself like this took all my strength. In went the needle and I howled and sobbed miserably, but tried in vain to keep still. I could see nothing because of the bandage. If only I could have seen the faces of my friends it might perhaps have helped me. But I was in the dark – a terrible darkness – with nowhere to look for consolation but within myself. It was late and we had all had more than enough.

From 'Annapurna, Mon Amour'
by Maurice Herzog

4
Avalanche

Here, climber Kurt Diemberger describes experiencing an avalanche in 1957 whilst climbing Mount Chogolisa in the Himalayas. The avalanche is started when a cornice – an overhanging edge of snow – breaks off and sends huge amounts of dislodged snow down the mountainside.

How quickly the clouds were coming towards us now! We hoped they wouldn't interfere with our view from the top. We quickened our pace. The last steep pitch began a little way up there, and close above it we could see the tower that was the summit – 1,500 feet at the most – *that* couldn't take so very long.

Presently a little cloud came climbing up the slope below us. It grew larger, enveloping us, enveloping the peak. Without any warning, all hell broke loose. Grey veils of mist scurried across the ridge. Unnatural darkness swamped us. We fought our way forward through clouds of blown snow, bending double to meet the fury of the gale. On the crest of the ridge it flung itself upon us in full blast, snatching at our clothes, trying to claw us from our footing. It was terribly cold and the needles of ice blowing down into our faces hurt savagely. We could only see the next yard or two ahead. We kept on changing the lead, struggling grimly upwards.

It didn't seem possible. I thought of the blue sky such a short time back. It had all been so quick. I had an uncanny feeling – hadn't exactly the same thing happened to the Duke of Abruzzi, quite close to the summit? Were we going to be robbed, too? Away with such stupid thoughts; it was only a few hundred feet, and we had *got* to do it.

It grew lighter for a moment, as the wind parted the driving clouds. We stood rooted, looking up to where the summit must be. There it was, near enough to touch, looming darkly above us. An instant later the wrack[1] had swallowed it up again.

The storm continued its horrific din. Laboriously we moved up, with a steep, bottomless precipice[2] below us, keeping close to the ridge crest. Everything was white now and we could hardly see.

We were at about 24,000 feet. Only another thousand to the summit-tower. Suddenly Hermann spoke: 'We've got to turn back at once, or the wind will cover our tracks up, and we shall stray out on to the cornices!' He was quite right. We hadn't given a thought to it; and now visibility was almost nil.

We should have to hurry. We turned then and there. Hermann had been leading, so I was in front now. He followed at a safe distance of ten to fifteen yards, which was all that visibility would permit.

Bent double, I felt my way downwards. It was incredible – only 150 feet down, there was no trace to be seen of our upward trail, except the deep holes made by our axes. Very soon there wouldn't be very many of *them*. And still the tempest kept up its infernal din.

I reckoned we must be at about 23,600 feet, and that we must be near the steep avalanche slope which had pushed us so close to the cornices. If only one

[1] **Wrack:** destructive storm

[2] **Precipice:** edge with very steep drop

could see a bit more! I turned and saw Hermann coming after me, keeping the distance unaltered, following in my actual steps. As I moved down, I kept looking across to the left, trying to see through the mist. All I could see was that it was getting a bit darker overhead and a bit lighter below. That must be the edge of the cornices. It seemed a safe distance away, but in mist distances can be deceptive. Perhaps it would be better to keep a bit to the right, but then I should have to look out for the precipice. It ought to be here by now. Ah, there's another axe-hole . . .

I looked anxiously to the left and then down to the surface at my feet. I was at a loss; it was almost impossible to see anything at all. *Crack!* Something shot through me like a shock. Everything shook, and for a second the surface of the snow seemed to shrink. Blindly, I jumped sideways to the right – an instant reflex action – two, three great strides, and followed the steep slope downwards a little way, shattered by what I had seen at my feet – the rim of the cornice, with little jagged bits breaking away from it. My luck had been in, all right! I had been clean out on the cornice. What would Hermann have to say about that, I wondered? I stopped and turned, but the curve of the slope prevented me seeing over the crest as I looked up. The light was improving a little. Hermann must bob up any moment up there. I still couldn't fathom that extraordinary shaking sensation; had the snow really settled under my weight?

Still no Hermann. 'Hermann!' I shouted. 'For God's sake, what's up? Hermann!' I rushed, gasping up the slope. There it was, the crest . . . and beyond it, smooth snow . . . and it was empty . . . Hermann . . . You! . . .

Done for . . .

I dragged myself up a little farther. I could see his last footmarks in the snow, then the jagged edge of the broken cornice, yawning. Then the black depths.

The broken cornice – that had been the quaking beneath my feet, then.

I couldn't get a sight of the North Face from anywhere near. I should have to get down to Ridge Peak for that. As I went down, the storm gradually abated, and the mists lifted from time to time. I was utterly stunned. How could that have happened just behind me? I had the greatest difficulty in getting up the short rise to Ridge Peak, but even before I got there it had cleared up. I hurried out to the farthest edge of the cliffs.

The storm was hunting the clouds high into the heavens. Above the veils of mist and through them a ridge loomed up – a tower – a great roof with tremendous banners of blown snow streaming from it. Chogolisa, the horrible. I could see the spot where we had turned at about 24,000 feet. Our trail down the broad snow-field below was crystal clear. Then that fearsome drop to the north – into the clouds. And there, even closer to our tracks as they ran straight downwards, the encroaching precipice*. And then I could see it all with stark and terrible clarity. Just at

* **Encroaching precipice:** as the avalanche falls it breaks away and takes bits of the mountain with it, reducing the distance between the edge and the climbers

that point, Hermann had left my tracks at a slight bend, where I was hugging the rim of the precipice, and gone straight on ahead, only three or four yards – straight out on to the tottering rim of the cornice – straight out into nothingness. Of the foot of the wall I could see nothing. Stupidly, I stared upwards again.

If we had been roped . . .

I looked down along the face, shuddering . . .

No, I should never have been able to hold him there; at the moment of his fall I myself was too far out on the overhanging snow.

At last I could see clearly down below, where the broad snow-masses of an avalanche fanned out. The crashing cornice had set it off and it had swept the face clean. Hermann was nowhere to be seen. He must have fallen at least 1,000, maybe 2,000 feet and was lying there buried under the piled-up snow. Could he have survived that? There was no answer to my shouts and I had no way of getting down there. I should have to fetch the others and we should have to come from below. That was the only faint possibility. I strained my eyes, searching every cranny, searching for a rucksack, a ski-stick, a dark blob. But there was nothing to be seen – absolutely nothing. Only our tracks – up there . . .

Clouds blotted the mountain out again. I was alone.

From *Summits and Secrets* by Kurt Diemberger

5
Trapped

Aron Ralston is famous for the way he solved a problem when he found himself in a life-or-death fix. His hand had been trapped between a rockface and a fallen stone, which wedged itself against the wall. Unable to move, he waited for help but no one knew he was there. In desperation, he finally decidedly to amputate his own hand to free the rest of his body and thus save his life. This extract describes the moment he found himself trapped.

Just below the ledge where I'm standing is a chockstone[1] the size of a large bus tyre, stuck fast in the channel between the walls, a few feet out from the lip. If I can step onto it, then I'll have a nine-foot height to descend, less than that of the first overhang. I'll dangle off the chockstone, then take a short fall onto the rounded rocks piled on the canyon floor. With one hand and one foot on each of the walls, I traverse[2] out to the chockstone. I press my back against the south wall and lock my left knee, which pushes my foot tight against the north wall. With my right foot, I kick at the boulder to test how stuck it is. It's jammed tightly enough to hold my weight. I step onto the chockstone. It supports me but teeters slightly. I squat and grip the rear of the lodged boulder, turning to face back upcanyon. Sliding my belly over the front

[1] **Chockstone:** a stone wedged in by other rocks
[2] **Traverse:** climb across

edge, I can lower myself and hang from my fully extended arms, akin to climbing down from the roof of a house.

As I dangle, I feel the stone respond to my grip with a scraping quake as my body's weight applies enough torque to disturb it from its position. Instantly, I know this is trouble, and instinctively, I let go of the rotating boulder to land on the round rocks below. When I look up, the backlit chockstone falling towards my head consumes the sky. Fear shoots my hands over my head. I can't move backward or I'll fall over a small ledge. My only hope is to push off the falling rock and get my head out of its way.

The next three seconds play out at a tenth of their normal speed. Time dilates, as if I'm dreaming. In slow motion: The rock smashes my left hand against the south wall; my eyes register the collision, and I yank my left arm back as the rock ricochets*; the boulder then crushes my right hand and ensnares my right arm at the wrist, palm in, thumb up, fingers extended; the rock slides another foot down the wall with my arm in two, tearing the skin off my forearm. Then silence.

My disbelief paralyzes me temporarily as I stare at the sight of my arm vanishing into a small gap between the fallen boulder and the canyon wall. Within moments, my nervous system's pain response overcomes the initial shock. My hand! The flaring agony throws me into a panic. I grimace and my mind commands my body, 'Get your hand out of there!'

* **Ricochet:** to bounce back

I yank my arm three times in a naïve attempt to pull it out. But I'm stuck.

Anxiety has my brain tweaking; searing-hot pain shoots from my wrist up my arm. I'm frantic, and I cry out loud. My desperate brain conjures up a story in which an adrenaline-stoked mum lifts an overturned car to free her baby. I'd give it even odds that it's made up, but I do know for certain that *right now*, while my body's chemicals are raging at full flood, is the best chance I'll have to free myself with brute force. I shove against the large boulder, heaving against it, pushing with my left hand, lifting with my knees pressed under the rock. I get good leverage with the aid of a twelve-inch shelf in front of my feet. Standing on that, I brace my thighs under the boulder and thrust upward repeatedly, grunting, 'Come on . . . move!' Nothing.

I rest, and then I surge again against the rock. Again nothing. I replant my feet. Feeling around for a better grip on the bottom of the chockstone, I reposition my left hand on a handle of rock, take a deep breath, and slam into the boulder, harder than any of my previous attempts. 'Yeearrgg . . . unnnhhh,' the exertion forces the air from my lungs, all but masking the quiet, hollow sound of the boulder tottering. The stone's movement is imperceptible; all I get is a spike in the already exaggerated pain, and I gasp, 'Ow!'

I've shifted the boulder a fraction of an inch, and it's settled onto my wrist a bit more. This thing weighs a lot more than I do – it's a testament to how amped I am that I moved it at all – and now all I want is to move it back. I get into position again, pulling with my left hand on top of the stone, and budge the rock back ever so slightly, reversing what I just did. The pain eases a little. In the process, I've lacerated and bruised the skin over my left knee. I'm sweating hard. With my left hand, I lift my right shirtsleeve off my shoulder and wipe my forehead. My chest heaves. I need a drink, but when I suck on my hose, I find my water reservoir is empty.

I have a litre of water in a Lexan bottle in my backpack, but it takes me a few seconds to realize I won't be able to sling my pack off my right arm. I remove my camera from my neck and put it on the boulder. Once I have my left arm free of the pack strap, I expand the right strap, tuck my head inside the loop, and pull the strap over my left shoulder. The weight of the equipment, video camera, and water bottle tugs the pack down to my feet, and then I step out of the strap loop. Extracting the dark gray water bottle from the bottom of my pack, I unscrew the top, and before I realize the significance of what I'm doing, I gulp three large mouthfuls of water and halt to pant for breath. Then it hits me: In five seconds, I've guzzled a third of my entire remaining water supply.

'Oh, damn, dude, cap that and put it away. No more water.' I screw down the lid tight, drop the bottle into the pack resting at my knees, and take three deep breaths.

'OK, time to relax. The adrenaline's not going to get you out of here. Let's look this over, see what we got.' Amazingly, it's been half an hour since the accident. The decision to stop rushing from one brutish attempt to the next allows my energy to settle down. This isn't going to be over quickly, so I need to start thinking. To do that, I need to be calm.

The first thing I decide to do is examine the area where the boulder has my wrist pinned. Gravity and friction have wedged the chockstone about four feet above the canyon floor at three spots. My hand and wrist form a fourth support where they are caught in the grip of this horrific handshake. I think, 'My hand isn't just stuck in there, it's actually holding this boulder off the wall. Oh, man, I'm dead.'

I reach my left fingers down to my right hand where it is visible against the north wall of the canyon. Poking down into the small gap above the catch point, I touch my thumb, which is already a sickly gray color. It's cocked sideways in the space and looks terribly unnatural. I straighten my thumb with the fore and middle fingers of my left hand. There is no feeling in any part of my right hand at all. I accept this with a sense of detachment, as if I'm diagnosing someone else's problem. This calms me. Without sensation, it doesn't seem as much my hand – if it were my hand, I could feel it when I touched it. The farthest part of my arm I can feel is my wrist, where the boulder is pinning it. Judging by appearances, the lack of any bone-splitting noises during the accident, and how it all feels to my left hand, I probably don't have any broken bones. From the nature of the accident, though, there is very likely substantial soft-tissue damage at the least, and for all I know, something could be broken in the middle of my hand. Either way, not good.

Investigating the underside of the boulder, I can touch the little finger on my right hand and feel its position with my left hand. It's twisted up inside my palm, in a partial fist; my muscles seem to be in a state of forced contraction. I can't relax my hand or extend any of my fingers. I try to wiggle each one independently. There's no movement whatsoever. I try flexing my muscles to make a tighter fist, but there isn't even the slightest twitch.

No one knows where I am. I failed to leave a detailed trip plan with a responsible person. Still eight miles from my truck, I am alone in an infrequently visited place with no means to contact anyone outside the fifty-yard throw of my voice. Alone in a situation that could very shortly prove to be fatal. It might take people a few days to figure out where I went, but there could be a search out by Wednesday, and if they find my truck, it wouldn't be long after that.

The major hitch is that I don't have enough water to wait that long – twenty-two ounces total. The average survival time in the desert without water is between two and three days, sometimes as little as a day if you're exerting yourself in 100-degree heat. I figure I'll make it to Monday night. If a rescue comes along before then, it will be an unlikely chance encounter, not an organized effort. In other words, rescue seems about as probable as winning the lottery.

By nature I'm an impatient person; when a situation requires me to wait, I need to be doing something to make the time pass. I don't sit still well. In my present situation, that's probably a good thing. I have a problem to solve – I have to get out of here – so I put my mind to what I can do to escape. Eliminating a couple ideas that are too dumb (like cracking open my AA batteries on the boulder and hoping the acid erodes the chockstone but doesn't eat into my arm), I organize my other options in order of preference: excavate the rock around my hand with my multi-tool; rig ropes and an anchor above me to lift the boulder off my hand; or amputate my arm. Quickly, each option seems impossible: I don't have the tools to remove enough rock to free my hand; I don't have the hauling power needed, even with a pulley system, to move the boulder; and even though it seems my best option, I don't have the tools, know-how, or emotional gumption to sever my own arm.

From *Between a Rock and a Hard Place*
by Aron Ralston

After having to cut off his own hand, Aron Ralston now has a prosthetic arm and hand.

At the Frontier

Explorers at the edge of the known world

6
Visiting a tree-house

Nick Middleton decided to spend some time in the three most difficult places in the world to survive, and to visit people who have made their homes in such difficult places. He chose to visit a remote jungle, a sand desert, an ice desert and, here, a remote swamp in Papua. The people live in tree-houses high above the swamp. The writer has vertigo: a fear of heights.

Late on the morning of our last day in Kenalua. John and I made our way down to the foot of the towering tree in question.

John, of course, hardly broke his stride to climb straight up the ladder right to the very top. I craned my neck to watch him disappear, looking hopefully for signs that the ladder was defective in some way, so giving me an honourable let-out from the exercise. But no such luck.

I'd talked this operation over with John, and decided that I would attempt to scale this impossible height only if he could take a rope up top, tie it to the tree, and throw it down for me to secure around my waist.

A tree-house in a swamp in Papua New Guinea.

John would then take up the slack as I climbed, providing some security against a fall. Naturally, this meant John himself would have to climb the ladder without any safety devices, but he wasn't fazed by this. His confidence had just been borne out, making me feel a little bit like a weakling. I consoled myself with the thought that having been brought up here, John had probably been climbing trees like this one, though possibly not quite so high, since he was a child. Whatever the rights and wrongs of this, he was now up there, having secured the rope to the tree, and I was still standing below, most definitely not up there.

I looked again, up towards John, who was now sitting nonchalantly on the tiny platform far above my head. This tree-house was a good thirty-five metres high. That's at least a hundred feet off the ground. It was way too high for my liking.

Strange things go through your mind when you attempt the impossible. For anyone who might think that the word 'impossible' is overstating the matter, let me explain. I'm not exactly afraid of heights, it's just that I'd rather avoid them. My problem lies in that perverse part of my mind that not only enjoys being high in the sky without much to hold on to, but actually delights in telling the rest of me so. Not only that, but this side to my personality, which normally lies dormant, becomes particularly rebellious when at altitude. The rebellion usually takes the form of suggesting that I throw myself off. So there we are. I'm not afraid of heights, but I'm terrified that I'll cast myself into the ether, just to see what it's like.

The first third of the ladder wasn't too bad. I'd checked the rope wound my waist several times before leaving the ground, and now found that the rungs were made of stout sticks and the rattan holding them was steady and strong. I talked my way up, telling myself that this wasn't really that difficult an exercise and that the Kombai made the ascent on a regular basis, so the ladder must be safe. All I had to remember was to hold on to it and everything would be fine.

Then I reached a large stick that marked the point where the first length of ladder was joined to a second.

I had to manoeuvre myself around it, which wasn't easy. 'Don't look down,' I told myself, but this was stupid advice because I had to look down to see where to place my feet. 'OK then, only look at your feet,' I said. 'Just don't look at the ground.'

The next stretch of ladder, the middle third of the climb, took me higher off the ground, a statement of the obvious, but I said it anyway to prove to myself that I was still on my side. Under no circumstances was I going to try and fool myself about this.

I stopped, probably half-way up, and told myself that I had done pretty well. 'Now, if you want to,' I said to myself, 'you can go back down.'

I hesitated, caught in two minds, which is not a good state to be in while standing half-way up a thirty-five-metre rattan rope ladder. I was veering towards a descent when John called down from on high.

'How're you doing there? The view from up here is fantastic.'

I looked around. The view was rather good from where I was standing, too, but maybe it was better still from up top. I climbed another rung.

'You're going up,' I muttered. 'You're going up to the top. Keep climbing. You're going up.' And my feet obeyed.

Two-thirds of the way up, the ascent became horrifying. Until this point, the ladder had been angled in towards the tree in the conventional manner, but its final third was vertical. I didn't like it. The tree-house suddenly seemed impossibly tall, but I knew that if I stopped now I'd be stuck, so I carried on.

The next step nearly launched me on an attempt at

unaided flight because the ladder swung violently and I just clung on, my back angled towards the ground. This was ridiculous and I was terrified.

'This ladder's going the wrong way!' I complained to John.

'It has to, to get over this branch and on to the platform here,' he cried. 'But keep coming, you're doing well. You're almost there.'

I moved up another rung and then another. I hated every step. Why was I doing this? I asked myself, it's pointless. Much against my better judgement, I stood still for a moment, taking a well-earned breather, part of me reasoned. It was a serious mistake. My left leg started shaking involuntarily. I looked down, just as far as the trembling limb, and nearly laughed. But only nearly. I was too petrified to find it amusing, and even if I had laughed, I'd have never heard it above the alarm bells ringing in my head.

'My leg's shaking,' I told John, who had now ceased to be a speck far above the ground and had regained his status as a real person. I could see the coil of rope tied to the top of the tree trunk behind him, my lifeline.

'Just keep coming,' he advised. 'You're almost there.' It was easy for him to say; rather less so for me to do.

'I suppose if I want to do a poo now,' I pondered aloud, 'I'll just have to do it in my pants.' John didn't have an answer to that.

There were only a few rungs left. My leg wasn't about to stop shaking while on the rung where I stood, so I thought I'd try the next one. Implementing this strategy took my leg's mind off the shaking.

'You really have almost made it,' John told me. He was right. If I'd stretched out my hand I could have touched his leg as it dangled down from the platform.

Somehow, I'll never know exactly how, I climbed the remaining rungs and eased myself across the narrow platform and into the tallest tree-house in the world. Inside, it looked just like Fiambo's, only higher.

From my position lying on my back on the floor, the only posture that felt even vaguely safe to my mind, I shook John's hand. 'Thanks,' I told him.

Incredible though Kenalua's tallest tree-house was as a piece of engineering, I spent no more than ten minutes inside it and I hated every one of them. The view that John had raved about was virtually identical to the one I'd seen while standing only half-way up the ladder. There were trees everywhere, and below them, no doubt, lurked a lot of swamp.

From *Surviving Extremes* by Nick Middleton

7
A meal in the Arctic

This is Nick Middleton again, this time invited to share a meal in the Arctic Circle.

The streets of Qaanaaq were not only littered and muddy that first day, but they were also pervaded by a powerful and very unpleasant smell. It seemed to follow me round as I walked, a pungent blend of rotting flesh underlain by the delicate aroma of dog.

Earlier, I'd checked the soles of my boots, but found nothing. As I approached the house that had been pointed out to me, a standard red wooden home surrounded by a gaggle of people eating and drinking, the stench grew stronger. It hung in the air like an invisible toxic cloud and by the time I came within earshot of the throng of people, the reek was almost overpowering.

I got talking to a middle-aged Danish woman on the edge of the gathering. Behind her, tables were spread with plates of small pancakes and lines of paper cups beside urns of tea and coffee. People were tucking in. I could just make out a red mass on the tabletop – source, it seemed, of the mysterious odour.

'This is as near as I can go,' she concluded.

'What is it?' I asked.

'A local delicacy,' she said. 'It's a seal stuffed with seabirds, "auks" I think you call them in English.'

Interesting, I thought to myself. But unusual though the ingredients were, I still couldn't decide why the smell was so awful.

'They remove the seal's innards,' she went on, 'and replace them with the birds, feathers and all. Then they bury the whole thing for a few months until it's ready.'

'They don't cook it?'

'Oh no, that's why it smells so terrible. The Inuit love it.'

There was movement behind her as I stood there taking in this information. An Inuit woman was talking to her and she translated. 'She says you are very welcome to try it if you like.'

My mind went into a spin. 'You don't have to,' she was saying, but the kind face of the woman behind her was gesturing me towards the bloody table.

'I don't want to deprive anyone of their lunch,' I said, trying to sound nonchalant but inside feeling increasingly desperate.

'Don't worry, they'd be happy for you to try,' she replied.

I had hoped that she might have been an ally, but she probably thought she was just trying to be helpful.

'I won't come with you,' she added as I moved off, holding my breath, in the direction of the appalling spread.

The table was covered with the bloody remains of rotting flesh and a few flies were busy gorging themselves on the entrails. Beside it, a cardboard box was filled with a mass of small bones and blood-spattered feathers, the remains of the auks that had filled the seal's cavity. Congealed blood and guts were everywhere, but to my intense relief it seemed that the platter was all but consumed.

'Oh what a shame,' I managed to stutter to a young woman standing beside the low table, 'I was looking forward to sampling some of this.' In my mind it was the most obvious lie I'd told in a long time, but my concentration was focused on other things. I was frantically trying to hold back my intense desire to vomit under the influence of the incredibly powerful stench.

The woman smiled. 'I'm afraid so,' she said with a slight American accent, 'but try some of this.' She patted a large chunk of flesh that sat on the table beside the disembowelled seal carcass.

'Thank you,' I said stupidly, and, 'What is it?' as she cut a thick slice from the lump with a large hunting knife.

'Narwhal liver,' she said.

To my eternal credit, I managed to swallow the portion of the rotting liver without throwing up, but I've never felt so relieved in all my life as when I thanked her and made my exit.

From *Surviving Extremes* by Nick Middleton

8
Exploring the sea bed

The deep oceans are still unexplored, but that has never stopped people from trying.

History

The ancient Romans had regiments of frogmen called *urinatores*. Knowing the habits of divers, perhaps the reason for this name should remain obscure. They certainly had odd habits, including going below with a mouthful of oil which they then spat out under water in order to 'catch a mouthful of breath', whatever that might mean.

It is Aristotle who records that sponge divers had inverted jars full of air lowered to them: 'These vases are forced steadily down, held perfectly upright, for if tipped slightly, the water enters.' Clearly, even in the fourth century BC the principle of the diving bell was understood. It was not, however, until 1599 that a large inverted cask with a man inside was successfully used under water. Edmund Halley, when not gazing at comets, designed a wooden bell large enough to carry several men to the sea floor. His idea was to extend the divers' endurance by sending down barrels of air to replenish the supply. He also provided a watertight hood and hose so that they could work outside the bell. Halley's bell became used for under-water work as much as 60 feet down and for 90 minutes at a time.

The traditional 'hard hat' helmet was invented by an Englishman, John Deane, in 1820. It was the first outfit that sealed off the diver from the elements and controlled the flow of air to him. The gear was so successful that in 1839 the Royal Navy founded the first ever diving school.

Jack Kitching

It was July 1931 at Wembury Bay on the Devon coast. The diver was dressed in a rugby shirt and shorts but as summer set in with its usual severity, he donned a woollen jumper, tweed trousers and stout walking shoes. It was as if he were going for a ramble over rock-strewn valleys, which I suppose he was.

On his head was a milk churn with a window inserted at the front, and 150 feet of garden hose attached to replenish the air. The lead weights that kept the helmet in place were so heavy that they could not be attached until the diver was submerged.

The diver was Jack Kitching, now 23 years old and a zoologist from Cambridge. Without a diving suit, it was difficult to withstand the cold for more than twenty minutes at a time, but, by working in shifts, he and his colleagues managed to put in an hour a day under water.

His diving helmet had an internal telephone, the microphone almost completely filled with wax and encased within a balloon to keep it dry. The intention was to dictate notes to the surface where they would be written down, but the message he most frequently transmitted was: 'More air! More air!'

From *Stars Beneath the Sea* by Trevor Norton

Jack Kitching prepares for a dive, Scotland 1937.

Breaking the Limit

Record breakers

9
The four-minute mile

Roger Bannister was the first person to run a mile in under four minutes in 1954. Two other runners ran alongside to help him to pace himself over the first part of the mile. The current record is 3 minutes and 43 seconds. No woman has ever run a mile in under four minutes.

There was a complete silence on the ground . . . a false start . . . I felt angry that precious moments during the lull in the wind might be slipping by. The gun fired a second time . . . Brasher went into the lead and I slipped in effortlessly behind him, feeling tremendously full of running. My legs seemed to meet no resistance at all, as if propelled by some unknown force.

We seemed to be going so slowly! Impatiently I shouted 'Faster!' But Brasher kept his head and did not change the pace. I went on worrying until I heard the first lap time, 57.5 seconds. In the excitement my knowledge of pace had deserted me. Brasher could have run the first quarter in 55 seconds without my realising it, because I felt so full of running, but I should have had to pay for it later. Instead he had made success possible.

At one and a half laps I was still worrying about the pace. A voice shouting 'relax' penetrated to me above the noise of the crowd. I learnt afterwards it was Stampfl's. Unconsciously I obeyed. If the speed was wrong it was too late to do anything about it, so why worry? I was relaxing so much that my mind seemed almost detached from my body. There was no strain.

I barely noticed the half-mile, passed in 1 minute 58 seconds, nor when, round the next bend, Chataway went into the lead. At three-quarters of a mile the effort was still barely perceptible; the time was 3 minutes 0.7 seconds, and by now the crowd were roaring. Somehow I had to run that last lap in 59 seconds. Chataway led round the next bend and then I pounced past him at the beginning of the back straight, 300 yards from the finish.

I had a moment of mixed joy and anguish, when my mind took over. It raced well ahead of my body and drew my body compellingly forward. I felt that the moment of a lifetime had come. There was no pain, only a great unity of movement and aim. The world seemed to stand still, or did not exist. The only reality was the next 200 yards of track under my feet. The tape meant finality – extinction perhaps.

I felt at that moment that it was my chance to do one thing supremely well. I drove on, impelled by a combination of fear and pride. The air I breathed filled me with the spirit of the track where I had run my first race. The noise in my ears was that of the faithful

Oxford crowd. Their hope and encouragement gave me greater strength. I had now turned the last bend and there was only 50 yards more.

My body had long since exhausted all its energy, but it went on running just the same. The physical overdraft came only from greater willpower. This was the crucial moment when my legs were strong enough to carry me over the last few yards as they could never have done in previous years. With 5 yards to go the tape seemed almost to recede. Would I ever reach it?

Those last few seconds seemed never-ending. The faint line of the finishing tape stood ahead as a haven of peace, after the struggle. The arms of the world were waiting to receive me if only I reached the tape without slackening my speed. If I faltered, there would be no arms to hold me and the world would be a cold, forbidding place, because I had been so close. I leapt at the tape like a man taking his last spring to save himself from the chasm that threatens to engulf him.

My effort was over and I collapsed almost unconscious, with an arm either side of me. It was only then that the real pain overtook me. I felt like an exploded flashlight with no will to live; I just went on existing in the most passive physical state without quite being unconscious. Blood surged from my muscles and seemed to fell me. It was as if all my limbs were caught in an ever-tightening vice. I knew that I had done it before I even heard the time. I was too close to have failed, unless my legs had played strange tricks at the finish by slowing me down and not telling my tiring brain that they had done so.

Roger Bannister smashes the record in 1954 by being the first person to run a mile in under four minutes.

The stopwatches held the answer. The announcement came – 'Result of one mile . . . time, 3 minutes' – the rest lost in the roar of excitement. I grabbed Brasher and Chataway, and together we scampered around the track in a burst of spontaneous joy. We had done it – the three of us!

We shared a place where no man had yet ventured – secure for all time, however fast men might run miles in future. We had done it where we wanted, when we wanted, how we wanted, in our first attempt of the year. In the wonderful joy my pain was forgotten and I wanted to prolong those precious moments of realisation.

I felt suddenly and gloriously free of the burden of athletic ambition that I had been carrying for years. No words could be invented for such supreme happiness, eclipsing all other feelings. I thought at that moment I could never again reach such a climax of single-mindedness. I felt bewildered and overpowered.

From *The First Four Minutes* by Roger Bannister

10
Returning home after sailing round the world

Ellen MacArthur was the youngest person and the fastest woman to sail around the world when she came second in the Vendée Globe race in 2001. The race ended at Les Sables d'Olonne in France.

Within the fog it was eerie. I could hear other boats around me, but all I could see through the grey denseness were the few square metres of dull water around us. The suspense gripped me. Small waves began to build as the wind increased, bringing a damp chill into the late evening air. My heart beat faster as with our growing motion my fears for the mast returned.

Although I was desperate to see everyone again and to cross the line before we had more problems, I still wasn't ready for the race to end. Our focus on getting here had been so intense that it was hard to see to the other side of it. I had been through the experiences in my head a million times, but at the end of it all, something somewhere inside me knew that everything was going to change.

Things began to happen more quickly. The support team were almost alongside us. The flashing white light of the buoy was getting closer and became clear ahead of me. For a brief moment there seemed to be complete silence – we were nearly there. I looked around *Kingfisher* for one final check that everything was still OK. As my eyes refocused on the buoy, there was a deafening crack . . . the gun had fired, and at 19:36 and 40 seconds on 11 February 2001 we had crossed the finish line.

Adrenalin surged through me. The support team pulled alongside us, its passengers jumping aboard like a raiding party, and as the horns blew and the voices screamed I was embraced and wrapped up in loving arms – my first human contact for over three months.

Strangely, there were no tears, just the most incredible feeling of relief. As if a plug had been pulled, my concentration ebbed away in the time it takes for a gun to fire. No longer did I need to sleep for just ten minutes to recover, no longer did I need to look at the instruments each time I blinked. It was over, the race was over, and if it weren't for the adrenalin I'm sure I would have collapsed. We had made it. Together, *Kingfisher* and I had made it.

People were cheering, waving and calling my name. Through the smoke from the flares I could see whole families, people old and young on the edge of the harbour walls and along the water's edge. In the distance I could see thousands of people hanging over their balconies. I'd never seen so many smiles at one time. Overwhelmed by the welcome, I could only smile back, from ear to ear. I tried to smile for every single face in that crowd as we slowly crept up the channel.

I was handed a pair of distress flares, which I banged on the deck to light. The heat was intense and the fumes filled the air. Through the red light of the flares I could see more, and made out the individual figures. 'THANK YOU ELLEN' was written on a piece of wallpaper held up by a boy and his mother – he was standing on tiptoe, trying to lift his message high in the hope that we would see it. People were waving flags and flares, there were scarves and torches. I felt every person in that crowd had been with us and that everyone there was sharing in the moment. It seemed as if I was enjoying a party, not a celebration laid on especially for us. I was smiling and cheering *with* the people.

The contrast from being completely alone to being surrounded by hundreds of thousands of people within a matter of hours, could not have been greater. It was such an intense situation that it was almost too much to bear. I wanted to jump high in the air to say thank you. The last time I had passed these harbour walls was

Ellen MacArthur celebrates her victory on her boat *Kingfisher*.

when we set off for the start. I remembered the nerves, the reality of the situation, and the concentration of trying to focus on the race that was about to start. Although I had to believe we would finish the race, I was aware of the dangers to come. Every one of the twenty-four boats crossed that start line with the hope of finishing. I found it difficult to comprehend that of all of those, I was just the *second* to make it. As I thought of what we'd been through together I dropped to my knees and kissed *Kingfisher*'s cold deck, the two flares still burning bright and hot in my hands.

Seconds out from the pontoon we had left on the day of the start, Mum and Dad came on board for the first time, their faces showing sheer happiness and relief. Dad walked across and held out his arms, and as they closed around me the length of time I'd been away was suddenly apparent. Mum hugged me too and as I wrapped my arms around both of them, she kissed me on my forehead . . . now I was home.

As *Kingfisher* finally approached the pontoon, I felt like a child awaiting an exam. All I could see were the hundreds of journalists, their lenses and microphones pointing directly at me. When we touched the dock moments later, I was standing completely alone.

I was oblivious to the noise and the hundreds of flashing cameras. How could I leave *Kingfisher*? How could I walk away? Our trip was over, and I knew deep inside that things never could or would be the same again.

I walked blindly to the cockpit. Never before in my life had I wanted to disappear like this. I stood facing *Kingfisher*'s bow and closed my eyes, my forehead pushing hard against her coach-roof. We needed time alone. I wanted to say thank you, I wanted her to know how sorry I was that it was all over, that I would have to leave her. Those few minutes felt like hours as I thought harder about one single thing than ever before in my life. Sadness felt so different from exhaustion. This was a pain in my heart, whereas before pain had only run through every bone in my body.

The last three months felt like forever and I could not remember what life had been like before the race. For the first time since I crossed the line my feelings were coming out, their rawness impossible to hide, I was about to leave my friend, and it was breaking my heart.

Deep down, I knew that I could not have done more to look after her. As I stood with my head bowed I could only say my last thank you as I heard the noise of the crowds once again. Just the fact that I was alive and standing with her was evidence enough to me that she had done her level best to look after me too.

Until this moment the finish had felt like a dream, the thousands of people, the yell from the crowds, and the bright lights continuously shining. But right now those images were blurred and distorted by the pain. I clenched my teeth and tore myself away.

I cannot remember those final steps to *Kingfisher's* side, but as I climbed over her guard wires for the first time in more than three months I felt as if I was leaving a very large part of me behind. As I jumped on to the pontoon, I held tight on to her wires, then laid my head against her. My eyes were tightly closed as

I reached out to stroke her hull, her rounded gunwale felt cool and calming, and for one last moment the world was closed off.

Then I heard the gentle words 'Come on, Ellen' as an arm slipped around me, and as I turned to leave my hand slid silently away from *Kingfisher*. Our Vendée Globe was over.

From *Taking on the World* by Ellen MacArthur

11
The conquest of Everest

In 1953, Edmund Hillary and Sherpa Tenzing became the first people to reach the summit of Mount Everest, the highest mountain in the world.

Above us the ridge continued on as before – enormous overhanging cornices on the right and steep snow slopes on the left running down to the rock bluffs. But the angle of the snow slopes was easing off. I went on chipping a line of steps, but thought it safe enough for us to move together in order to save time. The ridge rose up in a great series of snakelike undulations which bore away to the right, each one concealing the next. I had no idea where the top was. I'd cut a line of steps around the side of one undulation and another would come into view. We were getting desperately tired now and Tenzing was going very slowly. I'd been cutting steps for almost two hours, and my back and arms were starting to tire. I tried cramponing along the slope without cutting any steps, but my feet slipped uncomfortably down the slope. I went on cutting. We seemed to have been going for a very long time and my confidence was fast evaporating. Bump followed bump with maddening regularity. A patch of shingle barred our way, and I climbed dully up it and started cutting steps around another bump. And then I realised that this was the last bump, for ahead of me the ridge dropped steeply away in a great corniced curve, and out in the distance I could see the pastel shades and fleecy clods of the highlands of Tibet.

To my right a slender snow ridge climbed up to a snowy dome about forty feet above our heads. But all the way along the ridge the thought had haunted me that the summit might be the crest of a cornice. It was too late to take risks now. I asked Tenzing to belay me strongly, and I started cutting a cautious line of steps up the ridge. Peering from side to side and thrusting with my ice-axe, I tried to discover a possible cornice, but everything seemed solid and firm. I waved Tenzing up to me. A few more whacks of the ice-axe, a few very weary steps, and we were on the summit of Everest.

It was 11.30 a.m. My first sensation was one of relief – relief that the long grind was over; that the summit had been reached before our oxygen supplies had dropped to a critical level; and relief that in the end the mountain had been kind to us in having a pleasantly rounded cone for its summit instead of a fearsome and unapproachable cornice. But mixed with the relief was a vague sense of astonishment that I should have been the lucky one to attain the ambition of so many brave and determined climbers. It seemed difficult at first to

Sherpa Tenzing is photographed by Edmund Hillary when they become the first people to reach the summit of Everest, the world's highest mountain, in 1953.

grasp that we'd got there. I was too tired and too conscious of the long way down to safety really to feel any great elation. But as the fact of our success thrust itself more clearly into my mind, I felt a quiet glow of satisfaction spread through my body – a satisfaction less vociferous but more powerful than I had ever felt on a mountain top before. I turned and looked at Tenzing. Even beneath his oxygen mask and the icicles hanging from his hair, I could see his infectious grin of sheer delight. I held out my hand, and in silence we shook in good Anglo-Saxon fashion. But this was not enough for Tenzing, and impulsively he threw his arm around my shoulders and we thumped each other on the back in mutual congratulations.

But we had no time to waste! First I must take some photographs and then we'd hurry down. I turned off my oxygen and took the set off my back. I remembered all the warnings I'd had of the possible fatal consequences of this, but for some reason felt quite confident that nothing serious would result. I took my camera out of my pocket and then shuffled down the ridge a little so that I could get the summit into my viewfinder. Tenzing had been waiting patiently, but now, at my request, he unfurled the flags wrapped around his ice-axe and standing on the summit held them above his head. Clad in all his bulky equipment and with flags flapping furiously in the wind, he made a dramatic picture, and the thought drifted through my mind that this photograph should be a good one if it came out at all.

From *High Adventure* by Edmund Hillary

Surviving the Human Race

People who have survived the worst in other people

12
The First World War

A very large number of young men joined the army at the beginning of the First World War. The wages were good and they believed it was their duty to go to war. But most of them were not prepared for the horrors of war, and most of them died in it. Ronald Blythe did survive and these are his memories of the early days of the war.

We arrived at the Dardanelles and saw the guns flashing and heard the rifle-fire. They heaved our ship, the *River Clyde*, right up to the shore. They had cut a hole in it and made a little pier, so we were able to walk straight off and on to the beach. We all sat there – on the Hellespont! – waiting for it to get light. The first things we saw were big wrecked enemy guns, the second a big marquee. It didn't make me think of the military but of the village fêtes. Other people must have thought like this because I remember how we all rushed up to it, like boys getting into a circus, and then found it all laced up. We unlaced it and rushed in. It was full of corpses. Dead Englishmen, lines and lines of them, with their eyes wide open. We all stopped talking. I'd never seen a dead man before and here I was looking at two or three hundred of them. It was our first fear. Nobody had mentioned this. I was very shocked. I thought of Suffolk and it seemed a happy place for the first time.

Later that day we marched through open country and came to within a mile and a half of the front line. It was incredible. We were there – at the war! The place that we had reached was called 'dead ground' because it was where the enemy couldn't see you. We lay in little square holes, myself next to James Sears from the village. He was about thirty and married. That evening we wandered about on the dead ground and asked about friends of ours who had arrived a month or so ago. 'How is Ernie Taylor?' – 'Ernie? – he's gone.' 'Have you seen Albert Paternoster?' – 'Albert? – he's gone.' We learned that if 300 had 'gone' but 700 were left, then this wasn't too bad. We then knew how unimportant our names were.

I was on sentry that night. A chap named Scott told me that I must only put my head up for a second but that in this time I must see as much as I could. Every third man along the trench was a sentry. The next night we had to move on to the third line of trenches and we heard that the Gurkhas were going over and that we had to support their rear. But when we got to the communication trench we found it so full of dead men that we could hardly move. There was the most terrible stink and for a while there was nothing but the living being sick on the dead.

The trenches: the aftermath of a German shelling in the First World War.

I did sentry again that night. It was one-two-sentry, one-two-sentry all along the trench, as before. I knew the next sentry up quite well. I remembered him in Suffolk singing to his horses as he ploughed. Now he fell back with a great scream and a look of surprise – dead. It is quick, anyway, I thought.

On June 4th we went over the top. We took the enemy trench and held it. It was called Hill 13. The next day we were relieved and told to rest for three hours, but it wasn't more than half an hour before the relieving regiment came running back. The enemy had returned and recaptured their trench. On June 6th my favourite officer was killed and no end of us butchered, but we managed to get hold of Hill 13 again. We found a great muddle, carnage and men without rifles shouting God's name. Of the sixty men I had started out to war from Harwich with, there were only three left.

We set to work to bury people. We pushed them into the sides of the trench but little bits of them kept getting uncovered and sticking out, like people in a badly made bed. Hands were the worst; they would escape from the sand, pointing, begging – even waving! There was one which we all shook when we passed, saying, 'Good morning' in a posh voice. Everybody did it. The bottom of the trench was springy like a mattress because of all the bodies underneath. At night, when the stench was worse, we tied crêpe round our mouths and noses. The crêpe had been given to us because it was supposed to prevent us being gassed. The flies entered the trenches at night and lined them completely with a density that was like moving cloth. We killed millions by slapping our spades along the trench walls but the next night it would be just as bad. We were all lousy and we had caught dysentery. We wept, not because we were frightened, but because we were so dirty.

We didn't feel indignant against the Government. We believed all they said, all the propaganda. We believed the fighting had got to be done. We were fighting for England. You only had to say 'England' to stop any argument. We shot and shot. On August 6th they made a landing at Suvla Bay and we took Hill 13 again, and with very few casualties this time. We'd done a good job. The trench had been lost yet again, you see. When we got back for the third time we found a little length of trench which had somehow missed the bombardment. There were about six boys in it and we butchered them right quick. We couldn't stay in the trench, we had to go on. Then we ran into machine-gun fire and had to fall flat in the heather, or whatever it was. Suddenly my mate caught fire as he lay there. A bullet had hit his ammunition belt. Several people near jumped up and ran back, away from the burning man and the machine-gun fire. I could hear the strike of the gun about a foot above my head. I lay between the burning man and a friend of mine called Darky Fowler. Darky used to be a shepherd Helmingham way. I put my hand out and shook him, and said, 'Darky, we've got to go back. We *must* go back!' He never answered. He had gone. I lay there thinking how funny it was that I should end my life that night. Then my mate began to go off like a firework – the fire was exploding his cartridges. That did it! I up and ran.

From *Akenfield* by Ronald Blythe

13
Factory work

Two hundred years ago, industry was thriving in England. The great cities of the north were full of mills and businesses. But the conditions for workers were terrible. In 1815, a special commission was set up by the government to look into the matter. It kept a record of the evidence given by ordinary working people. This is the evidence of a 23-year-old factory worker in Leeds.

What age are you?
Twenty-three.

Where do you live?
At Leeds.

What time did you begin work at the factory?
When I was six years old.

At whose factory did you work?
Mr Burk's.

What kind of mill is it?
Flax mill.

What was your business in that mill?
I was a little doffer.

What were your hours of labour in that mill?
From 5 in the morning till 9 at night, when they were thronged.

For how long a time together have you worked that excessive length of time?
For about a year.

What were the usual hours of labour when you were not so thronged?
From 6 in the morning till 7 at night.

What time was allowed for meals?
Forty minutes at noon.

Had you any time to get your breakfast or drinking?
No, we had to get it as we could.

Do you consider doffing a laborious employment?
Yes.

Explain what you had to do.
When the frames are full, they have to stop the frames, and take the flyers off, and take the full bobbins off, and carry them to the roller, and then put empty ones on, and set the frame going again.

Does that keep you constantly on your feet?
Yes, there are so many frames and they run so quick.

Your labour is very excessive?
Yes, you have not time for anything.

Suppose you flagged a little, or were late, what would they do?
Strap us.

And they are in the habit of strapping those who are last in doffing?
Yes.

Constantly?
Yes.

Girls as well as boys?
Yes.

Have you ever been strapped?
Yes.

Severely?
Yes.

Is the strap used so as to hurt you excessively?
Yes it is . . . I have seen the overlooker go to the top end of the room, where the little girls hug the can to the backminders; he has taken a strap, and a whistle in his mouth, and sometimes he has got a chain and chained them, and strapped them all down the room.

What was his reason for that?
He was very angry.

Did you live far from the mill?
Yes, two miles.

Had you a clock?
No, we had not.

Were you generally there in time?
Yes, my mother has been up at 4 o'clock in the morning, and at 2 o'clock in the morning; the colliers used to go to their work at 3 or 4 o'clock, and when she heard them stirring she has got up out of her warm bed, and gone out and asked them the time; and I have sometimes been at Hunslet Car at 2 o'clock in the morning, when it was streaming down with rain, and we have had to stay till the mill was opened.

You are considerably deformed in person as a consequence of this labour?
Yes, I am.

And what time did it come on?
I was about 13 years old when it began coming, and it has got worse since; it is five years since my mother died, and my mother was never able to get me a good pair of stays to hold me up, and when my mother died I had to do for myself, and got me a pair.

Were you perfectly straight and healthy before you worked at the mill?
Yes, I was as straight a little girl as ever went up and down town.

Were you straight till you were 13?
Yes, I was.

Did your deformity come upon you with much pain and weariness?
Yes, I cannot express the pain all the time it was coming.

Do you know of anybody that has been similarly injured in their health?
Yes, in their health, but not many deformed as I am.

Is it very common to have weak ankles and crooked knees?
Yes, very common indeed.

This is brought on by stopping the spindle?
Yes.

Where are you now?
In the poorhouse.

State what you think as to the circumstances in which you have been placed during all this time of labour, and what you have considered about it as to the hardship and cruelty of it.

The witness was too much affected to answer the question.

Testimony of Elizabeth Bentley to the Parliamentary Commission of 1815

14
Locked up

Arthur Koestler was a journalist who found himself in prison in Spain during the Spanish Civil War.

Then I was taken to a cell.

For the first time I heard the sound of a cell door being slammed from the outside.

It is a unique sound. A cell door has no handle, either outside or inside; it cannot be shut except by being slammed to. It is made of massive steel and concrete, about four inches thick, and every time it falls to there is a resounding crash just as though a shot has been fired. But this report dies away without an echo. Prison sounds are echo-less and bleak.

When the door has been slammed behind him for the first time, the prisoner stands in the middle of the cell and looks round. I fancy that everyone must behave in more or less the same way.

First of all he gives a fleeting look around the walls and takes a mental inventory of all the objects in what is now to be his domain:

the iron bedstead,
the wash-basin,
the WC,
the barred window.

His next action is invariably to try to pull himself up by the iron bars of the window and look out. He fails, and his suit is covered in white from the plaster on the wall against which he has pressed himself.

He decides to practise and master the art of pulling himself up by his hands. Indeed, he makes all sorts of resolutions; he will do exercises every morning and learn a foreign language, and he simply won't let his spirit be broken. He dusts his suit and continues his voyage of exploration round his puny realm – five paces long by four paces broad. He tries the iron bedstead. The springs are broken, the wire mattress sags and cuts into the flesh; it's like lying in a hammock made of steel wire. He pulls a face, being determined to prove that he is full of courage and confidence. Then his gaze rests on the cell door, and he sees that an eye is glued to the spy-hole and is watching him.

The eye goggles at him glassily, its pupil unbelievably big; it is an eye without a man attached to it, and for a few moments the prisoner's heart stops beating.

The eye disappears and the prisoner takes a deep breath and presses his hand against the left side of his chest.

'Now then,' he says to himself encouragingly, 'how silly to go and get so frightened. You must get used to that; after all, the official's only doing his duty by peeping in; and that's part of being in prison. But they won't get me down; I'll stuff paper in the spy-hole at night . . .'

As a matter of fact there's no reason why he shouldn't do so straight away. The idea fills him with genuine enthusiasm. For the first time he experiences that almost manic desire for activity that from now on will alternate continually – up and down in a never-ending zig-zag – with melancholia and depression.

Then he realizes that he has no paper on him, and his next impulse is – according to his social status – either to ring or to run over to the stationer's at the corner. This impulse lasts only the fraction of a second; the next moment he becomes conscious for the first time of the true significance of his situation. For the first time he grasps the full reality of being behind a door which is locked from outside, grasps it in all its searing, devastating poignancy.

This, too, lasts only a few seconds.

'Let's see,' says the novice, 'where were we? Ah yes, that business of stuffing paper in the spy-hole. It *must* be possible to get hold of paper somehow or other.' He leaves the 'how' in this 'somehow' suspended in mid-air. This is a mode of thought that he will soon master – or, rather it will master him. 'When I get out,' he will say for example, 'I shall never worry about money again. I shall run along somehow or other.' Or: 'When I get out, I shall never quarrel with the wife again. We'll manage to get along somehow.'

Indeed, 'somehow or other' everything will be alright once he's free.

The fact that the prisoner follows this line of thought, which, as I say, is going, after a few days, to master him, means that the outside world increasingly loses its reality for him; it becomes a dream world where everything is somehow or other possible.

'Where were we? . . . Oh, yes, that business of stuffing paper in the spy-hole. Of course, somehow or other one can get hold of some paper. But is it allowed? No, it's certain not to be allowed. So why bother?. . .

'Let's take a more thorough inventory of the objects in the room. Why, look, there's an iron table with a chair which we haven't observed or fully appreciated yet. Of course the chair can't be moved from the table; it's welded to it. A pity, otherwise one might use it as a bed table, and put one's things on it when getting undressed – pocket-book, handkerchief, cigarettes, matches and so on . . .'

Then it occurs to him that he has neither pocket-book nor handkerchief, cigarettes nor matches in his pocket.

The barometer of his mood falls a second time.

It rises again the moment he has tried the tap over the wash-basin. Look, there's running water in prison – it isn't half as bad as one imagined from outside. After all, there is a bed (and it's much healthier to sleep on a hard bed), a wash-basin, a table, a chair – what more does a man need? One must learn to live simply and unassumingly: a few exercises, reading, writing, learning a foreign language . . .'

The next voyage of discovery is in the direction of the water closet. 'Why, there's even one of these – it's really not half so bad.' He pulls the plug. The chain refuses to function. And the barometer falls afresh.

It rises again once he sees he can fill the bucket with water from the tap and flush the lavatory pan in this way. It falls again when he sees that the tap has also ceased to function. It rises again when he reflects that there must be certain times of the day when the water runs. It falls – it rises – it falls – it rises. And this is how things go on – in the coming minutes, hours, days, weeks, years.

How long has he already been in the cell?

He looks at his watch: exactly three minutes.

From *Dialogue with Death* by Arthur Koestler

15
Surviving a nuclear attack

On Monday 6 August 1945 the Second World War came to an end when America dropped the first atomic bomb on the Japanese city of Hiroshima. 60,000 died and 100,000 were injured in the blast. Many more died later – and are still dying – as a result of radiation poisoning. The following year, an American magazine sent one of its reporters – John Hersey – to collect first-hand accounts of the bomb. This extract is about the experience of Mr Tanimoto, who was helping a friend to move furniture at the moment the bomb fell.

Pushing the handcart up to the rayon man's house was tiring, and the men, after they had moved their load into the driveway and to the front steps, paused to rest awhile. They stood with a wing of the house between them and the city. Like most homes in this part of Japan, the house consisted of a wooden frame and wooden walls supporting a heavy tile roof. Its front hall, packed with rolls of bedding and clothing, looked like a cool cave full of fat cushions. Opposite the house to the right of the front door, there was a large rock garden. There was no sound of planes. The morning was still; the place was cool and pleasant.

Then a tremendous flash of light cut across the sky. Mr Tanimoto has a distinct recollection that it travelled from east to west, from the city toward the hills. It seemed a sheet of sun. Both he and Mr Matsuo reacted in terror – and both had time to react (for they were 3,500 yards, or two miles, from the centre of the explosion). Mr Matsuo dashed up the front steps into the house and dived among the bedrolls and buried himself there. Mr Tanimoto took four or five steps and threw himself between two big rocks in the garden. He bellied up very hard against one of them. As his face was against the stone he did not see what happened. He felt a sudden pressure, and then splinters and pieces of board and fragments of tile fell on him. He heard no roar. (Almost no one in Hiroshima recalls hearing any noise of the bomb.)

When he dared, Mr Tanimoto raised his head and saw that the rayon man's house had collapsed. He thought a bomb had fallen directly on it. Such clouds of dust had risen that there was a sort of twilight around. In panic, not thinking for the moment of Mr Matsuo under the ruins, he dashed out into the street. He noticed as he ran that the concrete wall of the estate had fallen over – toward the house rather than away from it. In the street, the first thing he saw was a squad of soldiers who had been burrowing into the hillside opposite, making one of the thousands of dugouts in which the Japanese apparently intended to resist invasion, hill by hill, life for life; the soldiers were coming out of the hole, where they should have been safe, and blood was running from their heads, chests and backs. They were silent and dazed.

Under what seemed to be a local dust cloud, the day grew darker and darker.

***

Mr Tanimoto, fearful for his family and church, at first ran toward them by the shortest route, along Koi

Highway. He was the only person making his way into the city; he met hundreds and hundreds who were fleeing, and every one of them seemed to be hurt in some way. The eyebrows of some were burned off and skin hung from their faces and hands. Others, because of the pain, held their arms up as if carrying something in both hands. Some were vomiting as they walked. Many were naked or in shreds of clothing. On some undressed bodies, the burns had made patterns – of undershirt straps and suspenders and, on the skin of some women (since white repelled the heat from the bomb and dark clothes absorbed it into the skin), the shapes of flowers they had had on their kimonos. Many, although injured themselves, supported relatives who were worse off. Almost all had their heads bowed, looked straight ahead, were silent, and showed no expression whatever.

After crossing Koi Bridge and Kannon Bridge, having run the whole way, Mr Tanimoto saw, as he approached the centre, that all the houses had been crushed and many were afire. Here the trees were bare and their trunks were charred. He tried at several points to penetrate the ruins, but the flames always stopped him. Under many houses, people screamed for help, but no one helped; in general, survivors that day assisted only their relatives or immediate neighbours, for they could not comprehend or tolerate a wider circle of misery. The wounded limped past the screams, and Mr Tanimoto ran past them. As a Christian he was filled with compassion for those who were trapped, and as a Japanese he was overwhelmed by the shame of being unhurt, and he prayed as he ran, 'God help them and take them out of the fire.'

From *Hiroshima* by John Hersey

A man wheels his bicycle through Hiroshima, about 500 metres from where the bomb landed.

Messages from the Edge

The thoughts of people who have looked death in the face

16
Messages in bottles

Without a telephone or a postal service, shipwrecked sailors have been known to curl up letters and push them into bottles. These were then sealed and thrown to sea, in the hope that someone far away would pick them up and send rescue.

Messages placed in bottles have been known to float about for decades, even centuries. In sixteenth-century England, Queen Elizabeth I even appointed an official 'Uncorker of Ocean Bottles', making it a capital crime for any person to open bottles found in the sea or washed up. The fear was that some might contain secret messages from spies, not to mention the British fleet, who used this unlikely method to send messages about enemy positions ashore.

The strangest – and most tragic – case of a message sent seeking help was perhaps that of Chunosuke Matsuyama, a Japanese seaman who was shipwrecked with 44 shipmates in 1784. Shortly before he and his companions died of starvation on a Pacific coral reef,

Matsuyama carved a brief account of their plight on a piece of wood, sealed it in a bottle and then threw it into the sea. In 1935, 150 years later it washed up – at the very seaside village where Matsuyama had been born.

Certainly one of the saddest letters must be the one thrown by a passenger on board the torpedoed liner *Lusitania*, which sank in May 1915. According to one report, the message read,

> Still on deck with a few people. The last boats have left. We are sinking fast. Some men near me are praying with a priest. The end is near. Maybe this note will–

Matching it for sadness, perhaps, was the one found in March 1999 by a fisherman in the Thames estuary. In 1914 while crossing the English Channel, a homesick British soldier named Thomas Hughes wrote his wife a letter, sealed it in an empty ginger-beer bottle and tossed it overboard. Two days later, he perished in battle. The fisherman who found the note was flown to Auckland, New Zealand, and personally delivered the bottle to Hughes's 86-year-old daughter, who treasured it as the only letter she ever had from her father.

Not all messages found have such a bittersweet outcome, however. In 1948 a Russian fisherman found a message written in Norwegian and English. Once translated it made little sense:

> Five ponies and 150 dogs remain. Desire hay, fish and 30 sledges. Must return early in August. Baldwin.

It turns out that the polar explorer Evelyn Baldwin sent it in 1902, and he had returned alive and well!

One day in 1956, Martin Douglas kissed his wife, Alice, goodbye and set off in his small cabin cruiser for a day of fishing off the coast of Florida near his home. When he didn't return, air and sea searches swung into action. He was eventually declared 'missing at sea', and never seen again. About a year later, on an Australian beach, a jar was found with a note tightly sealed inside it.

> Should this note be found, please forward it to my wife, Mrs Alice Douglas, at Miami Beach, Florida. No doubt you're wondering what has become of me. I got blown out into the waters, due to engine trouble.

With the note was a blank cheque, on the back of which was the handwritten will of Martin Douglas.

But let's end things on a happy note. Paolina and Ake Viking were married in Sicily in the autumn of 1958, thanks to a far-travelling bottle. Two years earlier, Ake, a bored young Swedish sailor on a ship out at sea, had dropped a bottle overboard with a message asking any pretty girl who found it to write to him. Paolina's father, a Sicilian fisherman, picked it up and passed it to his daughter for a joke. Continuing the joke, Paolina sent off a note to the young sailor. The correspondence quickly grew warmer, Ake visited Sicily, and the marriage soon followed.

From *Sailing's Strangest Moments* by John Harding

17
Walter Ralegh's last letter

Sir Walter Ralegh had been a favourite of Queen Elizabeth I, but he was not well liked by the new king, James I, who imprisoned him and sentenced him to death. Ralegh wrote this letter to his wife Elizabeth in 1603, just before the time of his execution. As it happened, he was reprieved, and it was 15 more years before Ralegh was executed.

You shall receave, deare wief, my last words in these my last lynes. My love I send you, that you may keepe it when I am dead; and my councell, that you may remember it when I am noe more. I would not, with my last Will, present you with sorrowes, deare Besse.

Lett them goe to the grave with me, and be buried in the dust. And, seeing it is not the will of God that ever I shall see you in this lief, beare my destruccion gentlie and with a hart like yourself.

First, I send you all the thanks my hart cann conceive, or my penn expresse, for your many troubles and cares taken for me, which – though they have not taken effect as you wished – yet my debt is to you never the lesse; but pay it I never shall in this world.

Secondlie, I beseich you, for the love you bare me living, that you doe not hide yourself many dayes, but by your travell seeke to helpe your miserable fortunes, and the right of your poore childe. Your mourning cannot avayle me that am but dust.

I trust my bloud will quench their mallice that desire my slaughter; and that they will not alsoe seeke to kill you and yours with extreame poverty. To what frind to direct thee I knowe not, for all mine have left mee in the true tyme of triall: and I plainly perceive that my death was determyned from the first day. Most sorry I am (as God knoweth) that, being thus surprised with death, I can leave you noe better estate. I meant you all myne office of wynes, or that I could purchase by selling it; half my stuffe, the jewells, but some few, for my boy. But God hath prevented all my determinations; the great God worketh all in all. If you can live free from want, care for no more; for the rest is but vanity. Love God, and beginne betymes to repose yourself on Him; therein shall you find true and lastinge ritches, and endless comfort. For the rest, when you have travelled and wearied your thoughts on all sorts of worldly cogitations, you shall sit downe by Sorrow in the end. Teach your sonne alsoe to serve and feare God, while he is young; that the feare of God may grow upp in him. Then will God be a husband unto you, and a father unto him; a husband and a father which can never be taken from you.

Bayly oweth me two hundred pounds, and Adrion six hundred pounds. I beseech you pay all poore men. When I am gonne, no doubt you shalbe sought unto by many, for the world thinks that I was very ritch; but take heed of the pretences of men and of their affections. I am no more your's, nor you myne. Death hath cutt us asunder; and God hath devided me from the world, and you from me.

Remember your poore childe for his father's sake, that comforted you and loved you in his happiest tymes.

I cannot wright much. God knows howe hardlie I stole this tyme, when all sleep; and it is tyme to separate my thoughts from the world. Begg my dead body, which living was denyed you; and either lay itt att Sherborne if the land continue, or in Exiter church, by my father and mother. I can wright noe more. Tyme and Death call me awaye.

The everlasting, infinite powerfull, and inscrutable God, that Almightie God that is goodness itself, mercy itself, the true lief and light, keep and yours, and have mercy on me, and teach me to forgeve my persecutors and false accusers; and send us to meete in His glorious kingdome. My true wief, farewell. Blesse my poore boye; pray for me. My true God hold you both in His armes.

Written with the dyeing hand of sometyme thy husband, but now (alasse!) overthrowne.

Your's that was; but nowe not my owne,

W. Ralegh.

Portrait of Sir Walter Ralegh.

18
John Clare's end

John Clare was born in 1793 and died in 1864. He was a poet, which was unusual because he was not a well-to-do person as most poets were in those days. He was an ordinary man who lived in the countryside. He spent the last 27 years of his life in an asylum.

Letter to James Hipkins, 8 March 1860

Dear Sir,

I am in a Madhouse & quite forget your Name or who you are – you must excuse me for I have nothing to communicate or tell of & why I am shut up I don't know – I have nothing to say so I conclude

Yours respectfully
John Clare

I Am

I am – yet what I am, none cares or knows;
My friends forsake me like a memory lost:
I am the self-consumer of my woes –
They rise and vanish like oblivions host,
Like shadows in love frenzied stifled throes
And yet I am, and live – like vapours lost.

Into the nothingness of scorn and noise,
Into the living sea of walking dreams,
Where there is neither sense of life or joys,
But the vast shipwreck of my life's esteems;
Even the dearest that I love the best
Are strange – nay, stranger than the rest.

I long for scenes where man hath never trod
A place where woman never smiled or wept
There to abide with my Creator God,
And sleep as I in childhood sweetly slept,
Untroubling and untroubled where I lie
The grass below, above, the vaulted sky.

John Clare, 1860

19
What's the point?

John Diamond was a journalist who died in 2001. He wrote articles about his battle with cancer. Two months before he died, an editor asked him to write an article about the meaning of life from the point of view of someone facing death.

'Just tell me, John, what the hell is the point of it all?' said the e-mail from the editor.

And the answer is this:

This is what it's all about. It's about reading a paper on a Sunday morning while you're thinking about whether you can be bothered to go to the neighbour's New Year's Eve party tonight. It's about getting angry with me for having different opinions from yours or not expressing the ones you have as well as you would have expressed them. It's about the breakfast you've just had and the dinner you're going to have. It's about random acts of kindness which still, magically, win over acts of incivility or nastiness. It's about rereading *Great Expectations* and about who's going to win the 3.30 at Haydock Park. It's about being able to watch old episodes of *Frasier* on satellite TV whenever we want, having the choice of three dozen breakfast cereals and seven brands of virgin olive oil at Sainsbury's. It about loving and being loved, about doing the right thing, about one day being missed when we're gone.

And that's all it's about.

It is, above all, I suppose, about passing time. And the only thing I know that you don't is that time passes at the same rate and in much the same way whether you're going to live to 48 or 148. Why am I happy? Because I'm alive. And the simple answer to the question 'What the hell is the point of it all?' is this is the point of it all. You aren't happy? Yes you are; this, here, now, is what happiness is. Enjoy it.

From *Snake Oil* by John Diamond

John Diamond with his wife Nigella Lawson.